MONTAGE

DONOVAN LE'MEIR ATTERBERRY

"The Essentials Vendor Service LLC"

Cleveland, OH

ISBN-13: 978-0-578-41338-9

Printed in the United States of America

TABLE OF CONTENTS

TABLE OF CONTENTS

Montage: any combination of disparate elements that form or is felt to form a unified whole, single image, etc.

ACKNOWLEDGEMENTS

A sincere thank you to Jamille Smith on "Blood Ties". This piece occurred when a regular conversation transformed into an intellectual poetic dialogue. It was very organic and transparent so I thank you cousin for your contribution. Also I want to thank Ciara Herring for her dictation of the book. She gave an excellent interpretation of the current landscape most black men face coming up in an impoverished neighborhood. Lastly, I want to thank my family. Without your love none of this would've been possible.

And finally I want to thank you the reader for purchasing my first book. Please enjoy this intimate part of me dedicated to my late mother Cassandra Witten.

PRELUDE

To whom it may concern:

Memories are boxed, filed, and stored away. The emotional attach
-ments from these memories are only remnants contained within
our behavior of what really occurred. This makes us canvases; walk
-ing illustrations of experience and action. We are the incomplete
products of life, living a collage of what we desire to be. When you
strive for significance you can't ignore the tools that solidify your
signature. I've learned the residuals of life derive from the reactions
of the people it touches. I react without fear as I welcome you to my
painted canvas called Montage.

CHAPTER 1

WHEN UNADDRESSED PAIN IS ONLY
A TIME CAPSULE

- 1 in 3 women and 1 in 4 men have been victims of some form of physical violence by an intimate partner within their lifetime

- On a typical day, there are more than 20,000 phone calls placed to domestic violence hotlines nationwide

- 1 in 15 children are exposed to intimate partner violence each year, and 90% of these children are eyewitnesses to this violence

"Shut up!" was the first thing I heard. It was 1:00 am, and all I could hear was arguing. I assumed it was Marcus, my mother's boyfriend.

"Shut the fuck up, if you do what I tell you, this shit wouldn't be happening," Marcus said.

"This shit wouldn't be happening," I whispered to myself as I crawled out of bed.

I put my ear to the floor to hear what was going on below and I instantly heard my mother's voice.

"Marcus, please, don't do this."

My chest began to ache.

"Please, stop." I began to get up.

"PLEASE!!!"

I bolted down the stairs.

When I got to my mother's room, she was sitting on her dresser, staring at me while Marcus was choking her.

"Donny, run." She said weakly.

But I couldn't move. I was cemented by the fact that my mother was losing consciousness. He was killing her. Suddenly, Marcus looked at me and stopped. He walked towards me and said something that haunted me for years.

He said, "There is nothing you can do, so take yo black ass back upstairs and play your fucking games." Then he turned his back, closed the door, and my mother began to scream.

That night, I stayed awake until the house fell silent. I allowed my mind to drift and embrace whatever thoughts could console me. Eventually, I was found.

IN MY SLEEP

Murder is simplistic by design

The cover up is the only scenario that entails intricacies that persuade
the psyche

"I said grab the cinder blocks and align the bottom of the body bag"

See majestically I feel inclined to provide insight between crazies and
getaways

The moment you decide to commit

to the lush splash of blood reflecting your intent

is as important as the reluctance to over indulge with each blow

"Now place the body on top of the blocks"

Crimes of passion are sinful by nature clear indicators are
Excessive violence & mutilation

But the key to survival is to fall in love with the fact they can no
longer enjoy the pleasantries of life as we know it

I always envisioned it this way...to bury you is tedious but necessary
to find the freedom I fictionally display

MY DOMESTIC DISPUTE

The physical onslaught cannot appear because of the masquerade

The mask portrays the image it desires you to see

Underneath is the disease

The festering flesh eating depression that develops

when you don't believe

It tells you "YOU CANNOT LEAVE"

Shackled and subdued by the desire to be loved

You ignore the obvious

Dim lights that reflect off bloody wrists type of ambiance

This some crazy shit

Midnight sleep interruptions

No boogey man because monsters premeditate

Evil niggas are abrupt no sit up and wait discussions

Only blows and concussions

I was 11 with suicide attempt number one

Sickening as I think

Watching my mother a strong black woman succumb to a man

that's weak

But like they say you emulate what you see

Now I'm 25 with more than 10 occurrences of me getting my ass beat

by a woman who says "She loves me"

It's a cyclic tradition of forgiving and forgetting

Hoping and wishing

Damn! I'm trying to change you but along the way

my identity came up missing

"So what am I?"

A man trying to appease the ideal of a home that I never had

Or am I my mother trying to live my present

through the trials of my past

I guess I'm just dead, I guess this is it

Because I promise if I strike back I won't miss

Then what...I'm just another nigga beating

on another mother and shit

This is my dispute

My domestic violence

And fuck all the naysayers who think a nigga getting

slapped up is childish

I choose self over you praying to God I never hit u

JUST US CENTER

Let's see what's on the docket

Young and accused of what you assume is criminalistic

Not a filter to decipher what's bullshit

You operate with stereotypical clichés that positions me under

the convenience of your pen

See you wasn't there when she manipulated me

When she used our kids against me

See your interpretation is misguided because your privilege

makes you one sided

I didn't marry before I had my angels

I adopted her,s had two and took care of them

when I didn't have too

See real shit

My disparity derives towards a system that eliminates the

father for bullshit charges

Deeming him "HIGH RISK"

Positioning our children as cash cows

While the state reaps a cool cut of child support

No offense to the system that delegates what you

and yo baby daddy couldn't

But you didn't need Mr. Michael Kor as your clutch

When the man that bought it always came through in the clutch

Facing charges over you

While still full time in school

And working a 9-5 because you said the money you get

ain't enough for them to get school shoes

See this is the asinine ways of black women these days

Treating the ones that want to be fathers like slaves

As the white man dangles custody like freedom

I finally see it...most of y'all fighting inner demons

by shitting on us

BUT who really losing?

I bet the kids in the other room is what I'm assuming

ME VS YOU

See me and you been going through violent episodes

where you hit me and I think about hitting you

With 3 sets of eyes with the same hue

Observe not with the peripheral view

The irreversible acts is the proof

Or can you remember?

I swear your mental disconnect is equivalent to the

normality of its consistency

Meaning! You deal with life by going off on me

Just to let me know when compared where you've failed

I prevailed

Its resentment accumulated overtime

With intermissions devoted to sexual encounters

that lack the same intensity

A couple years my senior I was only naive

While you were the dreamer

Thinking like the chicken "if I could only cross the road"

but there's no other side

It's only you, your past, and a couple pills that

brings "the us" in you to a present view

Crazy thing is it's not just my two

yours call me Daddy now too

So what you wanna do?

Give up on yourself? Or rebirth to something new?

WHEN ABSENT OF ACTION WORDS WILL HAVE TO SUFFICE

My love was an imitation

A falsified claim with inabilities enshrined oversight

A hindrance in my view

Now exempt from my acknowledgement

I acknowledge the criticism I couldn't take

No longer the blame game

But the Mutumbo finger wave

As every communication remains blocked

Sometimes I reach with no intent of retrieval

But the upheaval of skeletons that lack the emotional nourishment

to revive the point in which we lapsed

Quickly we detach

With too many lines crossed

I forgot my Ts' and only seen the I's

I was financially giving and I was emotionally selfish

And I wish my love for you was more selfless

Because I self-sabotaged us and forfeited loves blessing

SAPIOSEXUAL

Premature my shallow was deep enough to tread

Only intrigued by what I can see

Neglectful to the hindsight attached to the interactions of life

A preverbal notion of wrong vs right

With a shift in insight and

Now my intrigue doesn't have a physical slight

But I have a new plight

See the intellectual prowess that digs into my psyche

is my new erection

Especially when my interests peaks

It's like a mind fuck I don't want to cease

The flow of conversation has me weak

How exactly do u get me after one meet? It's a puzzle piece fit

How my thoughts begin with me and end in you

It's only right though that you're too far and exempt from

physical touch

So for now I'll settle for a mental fuck

NOT YET REMOVED

The momentum is a mood shift

A trend to transition season is seasonal at best

Because neither party

Wants to leave so the party continues exempt from the motivation

that brought y'all there from the beginning

Yet you still feel his eyes in the midst of the children and the lies

So you concede to his fascination entirely with the simple things

The way you dress

The way you do your hair

Even your smell is to appease

Though the relationship is done

The physicality possesses its own greed

A playing field where it's you vs his team

Your willingness to love against his reluctant tendencies

My mama always said trust a zebra brandishing their stripes

Because fucking him now will not change his perspective overnight

I see the plan is to entice a conversation that alters the course

the relationship chose

But complacency is more evident than what was orchestrated

Y'all didn't choose each other

Y'all chose to party & bullshit

Now the party is over

And you ain't leaving with who you came with

THE PICTURES I PAINT

I'm staring at your soul

And it's scary to know I hold the fluidity of its existence

Observing your essence from the marble foundation in which I sculpt

I exhaust all my efforts into your depiction

Feverishly trying to mirror your beauty

But yet craft you to mold only to me

Similar to the Mona Lisa piece only the artist knows the truth

The outline of your conscious

Coinciding with your aura is honey dew

So sweet it is to be you

That a replica isn't feasible

I'm staring at your soul

And it's scary to know I hold the fluidity of its existence

This is my chance to capture you I hope I don't miss it

TELEPATHY

"Even without me I'm with you"

Is a statement that crystallizes properties you

never can really see through

Even with you in the rear view

The telepathy is reminiscent

As I try to explain my mental dilemma to a female

Jidenna I'm Bambi

Yet I still try to see through

"Even without me I'm with you"

Is a mind fuck that's intention is for me to get it

Like a warm sensation over my brain as I

envision your eyes piercing mine

I can feel you shuffling through as I hide the child in the king

from the Dreamcatchers jaws

Don't engulf what you already know

"Even without you I still feel you"

And this mental telepathy couldn't ring more clearly

Because even now I can't see through the crystal

The properties inside have become a veil over my eyes

as I revert back to the normality of the process

and I guess I just like you reading my mind

Even when you're not in sight

Sometimes life doesn't have meaning in the moment

CHAPTER 2

———————— ⚜ ————————

THE DEEPEST ABYSS COMES FROM LISTENING
TO THE DEVIL'S LIPS

THE DEPARTURE

The disparity of my thoughts are always evident after hours

A momentary inconsistency that lapses between relevancy and reality

But this moment isn't that

You're very much at the door

And even with it shut you still think it's appropriate to try a key

Yet she answers without acknowledgement of me

I think "Why the fuck are you here" I'm not expecting pleasantries

Based upon our last encounter when you manipulated me into

restraining myself from who you are... A coward

"You want to fight?"

Is your best claim

Very much so, only to prove that I'll never be you

"Move San"

"Move Ma" I reply with urgency

Steadfast it doesn't weigh as my mother states

"You are no longer welcomed here. Your stuff has been thrown out

and it's time for you to leave our lives for good."

A momentary consistency has lapsed between relevancy and reality

With that moment being everything

I found myself confused

Life without torment was very new

DIALOGUE

When my mother left Marcus, it didn't feel temporary like it once did. It felt permanent, and her life reflected it. She became heavily active in church, got married, and started to pursue her entrepreneurial goals. Life was better for her and the family as a unit. The continuity was infectious as we began to blossom in our own individual ways. But, like many people before her time; time is as relevant to the creator as the agenda you have for it.

February 2007,

"Donny!" My mother bellowed. "Ya, ma," I replied.

"Boyyy!" She growled.

"I'm coming, ma." In my most annoyed voice.

When I walked into the living room, my brother and sister were already sitting on the couch with her. Things looked normal. But, something felt off, like the air was sucked out of the room and unconsciously, we all needed air but forgot how to breathe.

"Sit down! I need to tell y'all something."

"Okay okay, what's up?"

At this point, I'm thinking who the fuck snitched? But, I didn't see any weaponry within her reach. So, what did we do?

My mother appeared strained, yet focused. I wasn't ready, but I was prepared for whatever was next.

"I have cancer, baby."

As the words escaped her psyche, she wasn't talking to my unknowing siblings. She was speaking directly to me. Like she knew this would affect me the most.

"Donny" my mother said softly.

I couldn't grasp the words, let alone respond at the moment. "You're going to die" is all I could muster.

Don't ask me how, but I guess I knew, and as the anger filled my spirit...I began to withdraw. My mother was lost in my eyes. She left Marcus, finished school, got saved, was buying a home and started a business...But it wasn't enough, cancer was still winning. It was winning the entire time.

MAMA

Conceding is the reliance on material possessions to cope

Utilizing women for an insatiable need

The urge to breathe in the demeanor which is you

This is nothing new when my hue only resembles you

So, tell me mother, what am I suppose to do?

I'm losing sight in this attempt to forget

"Remember this?"

Becomes a subtle notion

Because distance from pain shelters the disbelief of what occurred

A disassociation from what's relative

In fear of seeing a pure resemblance of your spirit

Punishing anyone that can't achieve it

Can you believe it?

That I've ignored the you in me for something I'll never see

No one will ever love like you

No one will ever understand like you

No one will ever know like you

So I apologize for adolescence in your time of need

The disgruntled aggression to be gratuitous

Cost a relationship that never came close to its maturity

So forgive me

For being recurring

Not acknowledging history

That grandma died too

During a teenage feud

DIALOGUE

The decline of my mother's health was a spiral of emotion. One minute, she was here, and then the next, she wasn't. Her last words were as precautious as the cancer ravaging her body.

"I love you, Donny, kiss the kids for me."

"Alright, ma, love you too. See you tomorrow."

And that was it...the morning of March 26th, 2007, she passed. But, even in death, she didn't disappoint. My sisters' birthday is March 25th, and she refused to be mourned on their day. She held on for them, and for that, we're all forever grateful. What I learned during this time is that the hardest moments aren't actually the death. It's the transition beyond the routine that's been established with the deceased. I didn't know a life without my mother. None of us did. What made matters worse was the funeral. I literally had to watch a countless number of individuals recount personal experiences they had, how they should've been there more, and how my mother was the greatest individual they've ever encountered. Exaggeration doesn't begin to describe the utilization of endearment that simply doesn't apply to the present. All I heard that day was excuses, lies, and bull-shit. My heart was cold towards my relatives because they were never there, and when I asked why, my mother was always the blame.

BLOOD TIES

Part 1

I'm a wordsmith

I create visual artifacts of my lifetime to be seen today

I stare in the mirror

Gaining the perspective of a person without a purpose

Searching endlessly in a vast abyss for my origin

But I only find hazy memories of life and death

Something like a sweet & sour effect

How breathless is the word "family"

Lingering in the air as it leaves my lips

Only knowing my mother joined to the hip

Ignorant to the dispute that hangs heavy like a mist

Or debris after a crash...

As planes collide...the explosion...the blast It's a free fall as

hope drops from the skies

But all boys grow old and so did I

The spelling of my name brought questions like a child

watching his parents' slain

Why me?

Why are we apart?

Did I do something wrong?

No I didn't

Because ignorance is bliss living behind a veil and not seeing

things for what they are

Which is shit

All the actions that make kin significant I missed

The identity of a person is molded from the foundation of

the upbringing one has

So without stability even Gods greatest creation

MAN...WILL FALL

Thus so did I, with one thought in mind where is my family

I think they left me behind

Part 2 - Response by Jamille Smith

My young bleed...you were never left...just lost Unseen,

for the cost of broken family ties, makes a tug of war impossible

The biggest obstacle you face...is the mirror

And I understand why long forgotten thoughts are hazy

But I hope our conversations make things clearer

See in you I see me...

Molded from a pen that ink flows through your blood...

Just one family tie...in love

See the news of an untimely passing, had the whole family gasping for

air and the answers!

But it's like we drew the short straw and a relationship that was

flawed never had a chance to heal

A choice to be still for there is always tomorrow...

Unless tomorrow never comes.

So living for today had us numb...to what you felt

No UNO but it's the hand we were dealt...so we can't "skip the past"

"reverse it", or "draw too" a conclusion...our days are

"numbered"...and living "wild" made us reckless.

I can't expect you to accept this as face value

But know my young bleed...we bleed the same blood, and lost just

means that someone was looking to find you!

Part 3

Drip splat as my blood leaks to the concrete

The anguish in me runs deep

False encouragement from outreached hands I find security in my

DNA addiction

Swallowing bottles to fill what's hollow

I substitute the average for what's not admired

Awaiting my real teachers arrival

Who is the man without the child?

Who is the child without the man?

I thought since his absence I had fam

But through the jungle of deceit, misfortune, and the people

who can see but won't speak

Somewhere we lost reality and became Israel

Searching for years for what is in plain sight

Ignoring the camaraderie that comes with blood ties

We click up, pick and choose who to tolerate and show affection

Only to widen the gap of relation between generations

Its' torment to be damned by your own kind and the crime

committed you didn't witness or take part but you still serve time

As you await your release

You reach...look...and hope...to be set free

So I pray for solace in something I've never known

A family.....a family to welcome me home

Part 4 - Response by Jamille Smith

Thoughts that flow freely but far and wide are the needy

hearts of a family

Torn apart by lies and greedy hearts

We all played our part

Some starred and others had a role

But the damage has been done

And we the children are now grown

Free to choose paths, not based on the past

but the needs of the present

This is how kings become kings from peasants

The relevance of the lives lived before is evident

But in fact it sets a precedent

For what we now lack and Need

As we grow to plant seeds...of our own

Make it known that this is all fam and all love

For those that we lost now look from above

In hopes that WE get it right

Understanding that mistakes are a part of life

Learn from it, it's all a process

Though it may be hard to digest drink it all in

Indulge in your family sin, think about it....beginning again

Part 5

And as I swallow I gulp the pain relinquish my thoughts

Open my eyes and embrace what I see

The division is self-inflicted and accepted

Never run because in most cases you won't be chased

The ignorance of possibility is thinking everyone is understood

So I assume their actions relay what they feel

But it's only a mental detour from acknowledging their

immovable behavior

A behavior that's afraid to be real

Chances are like steel without an eyeable flaw

But add the extreme pressures of emotion and it to will break

Now can you see the fracture?

A family that can face adversity and fight back without detachment

Here's the rapture

Knowing that the screams wasn't in vain And from a distance

you still know my pain

Family is not far from God

So I forgive what I don't understand and wait for the rest to subside

FRIKË
(pronounced freak)

———— ❧ ————

Unheard misery that does not have a barrier of time or distance

Reaching into the present from the past

Unrecognizable like a superhero in plain clothes

It strikes when you're vulnerable and injects the deadliest

venom of all....FEAR

Attacking the infrastructure of character and morale

Tormenting your soul into submission

Giving not an inch to reason

Only absolutes

Breaking spirit and stride

Leaving victims impassive and numb

Sucking the nectar of life from underneath

With only feelings of beguile

The light fades

And fear succeeds

The only question for the captive would be...

Will you forget everything you were taught to believe and concede?

If so you'll be living the same misery

BERLIN

My mind is cluttered

And poetry is the antidote to poison of thought

Different variables, chances, possibilities and no control of outcome

I pray for magnetism....that the drawing of the path comes

underneath my feet and I can walk without worrying

about what the finish may be

The distance seems continuous and forever within the horizon

But I know through faith I will watch this period of time fade and be

an addition to the stories that have made me great

Pain is only a momentary eclipse to who I am

A shadow that blocks light and builds character that will

sustain any shortcomings ahead

And as I breathe I know this confidence isn't all in my head

I draw from experience

When the odds against me were concrete without a cleft

The only challenge to breaking down the barrier was

pinpointing the weakness

The thought of change is the spark that ignites the fuse

And Berlin begins to fall

Merging the contents once contained

I introduce myself to my other side and commence brotherhood

instead of self-genocide

And walls don't exist anymore

My mind is still cluttered

But at least my conscious is free

Even in death, pain will not darken the light in me

IN MY SLEEP

Burying you only unearths demons of old

Hatred that's slithers into control

A venom symbiote without the hero

"I can't breathe"

"It's only the pain of forgotten flesh."

The stench is unfamiliar because I never dug this deep

Scar tissue that reopens when faced with identical intensity

Yet I don't bleed, but my body still confesses

what I eerily know is true

You can't bury your second like your first

"This one hurts Donny.

Now listen to me, eventually everyone leaves.

But the emotions they leave you with is

no longer their responsibility.

This is your pain now.

Your suffering. And you have to choose the progression

of your life from this moment."

"I'll dig deeper"

And with the erosion underneath my fingernails

My acceptance is burial and betrayal to self

An omission of truth

In order to forget you I have to become something new

CHAPTER 3

CONFIDENTLY SHALLOW

MY TRUTH

If I had to tell the truth, I would do it

in an interrogation room

Bright lights

Stale coffee

And a guy saying over & over again, we got you

Russian roulette with my lies as they may hit or miss

I kiss my alter ego for the haven he provides

to conduct all my crimes

Truth is, I've been more intrigued that someone hasn't gained

enough interest in me to seek the real me

It's so nonchalant as they pound the table and

state they have proof

But the best thing about lies there's no DNA to lose

So I chuckle & chide and say,

"All jokes aside, I'm an open book"

The reality is every statement whether false or true

has a underlining testament

That backtracks to the personality of its conductor

And just like a moving train,

once you concede to the rapid speed of infidelity to oneself,

you have to embrace it

Even when the momentum you're carrying

will not make the curve

I've yearned a listening ear some empathy

to my disability of honesty

If the audio is running let me confess that

its understanding I seek

I wouldn't lie when the tables' are turned on me

They don't believe and neither do I

Once you commit to the lie you must finish the story accordingly

And feel the patches with actions that you deem as true

The key is...to believe in yourself succumbing to your subconscious

to the bullshit you vomit

And hopefully you'll get a pass

Because these cops got that look and jail ain't for my light ass

SOCIAL DATING

It's almost a rude inclusion

Mandatory double dates exempt from

The physical standard

Flashing lights attached to *BINGS* that notify you of notifications

that can wait

Yes! It's the simplicity of our lives that made your ex cry when

your darting eyes forgot sex to read a text

While this nigga out of breath you're already on to what's next

Being accessible in the 21st century has made us easy

A bargain deal that still negotiates when likes are applied

I hate social media eyes but the attention when you lacking

is what gives you the backing

To do that little shit with yo foot

Yo ass pokes out

And I find myself trying to decide to comment or not

It's a rude inclusion to date you and who you pretend to be

But it's the irony of being attracted to what was advocated

The main reason why me and you had to meet

DOPE SICK

———————— ❧ ————————

This momentary displacement doesn't achieve an antidote

See I'm somewhat like an addict

As I filter through hypodermics for a fix

An adrenaline rush that's similar to a kiss

Is only a notion that when I apply pressure

Within your standards....you'll give me a hit

The significance becomes an abyss

When we miss

A call...A text

Or a moment to redirect the stress of life towards unconditional bliss

See me and you are eternal

A burning infirmary that can dismiss any detrimental ailment that

seeks US to cease

The only separation is the disconnect

So I filter through hypodermic memories

Hoping I don't rummage through us...&....miss our last hit

Because "I know" like Jay Z's American Gangster

You missing the D

& rehab wasn't for me

You're the antidote to lost hopes and dreams

Love so infectious it's a desired disease

I been doing you for so long I'm convinced without you

there's no me

DONNY LOUD

I'm genetically inclined to overdue the minimums

So much so food isn't a necessity

I'm Houdini

The escapee from reality towards inebriated clarity

Sides with me all too well

The functioning junky junction never threatens my mobility

tho I still work, raise my children, & conduct classes for the masses

on the back of accolades in which I lack passion

Thus, I'm undeterred with thee incentive to suppress

By utilizing haikus like

"Just enough to knock the edge off" At 11am ain't cool

See these are the junky rules

Blue collar fathers that you admire

Don't expire because the momentum is self-inflicted

To navigate through pitfalls before we start winning

Because Jordy was the blueprint of combining the two

Drugs & business...I'm a wolf on wallstreet too

I AIN'T SHIT

You ain't shit

Love proposals with a lusty haze

Ain't no different from the competition

At least them niggas is honest when they ditch em

You ain't shit

Because you like to infiltrate

Emotional tie people to your temporary feeling

It's overwhelming when you hit em

They tend to forget what shouldn't be forgiven

You ain't shit

No one's winning across the board

When inconsistent lies perpetuate concrete truths

You don't love her but you still fuck her

You hate the situation that you instigate

Childish games as you finger wave

You ain't shit

Pick a side, Who will be the victim this time?

Because with you in the middle and them on the outside

you punish all sides - I AINT SHIT

LERNAEN HYDRA

———— ❧ ————

Two faced and wicked I live within trinkets of humility

That rarely see daylight

Only by name does the sanctity show

Yet entitled to the lie that lives within the creator

Lines become blurred

As I track my dirty feet back & worth

Welcoming a voice to say "Stop" I admit!

I need an intervention

Because oddly enough I've conditioned my circle to

refrain from criticism

To the degree that skepticism is a reach

While I perfect an agenda that minimizes the damage of a choice

that shouldn't be just for me

I feel cold when Cole said

"I'm a fake nigga and it's never been clearer"

To the degree I don't practice what I preach

Really like the real shit is conclusive to my eyes only

While my heart shifts loyalty towards desires that only appease me

I forget I'm tracking through

So that means you see the bullshit too

Say stop so this all will ring true

And it isn't that easy to play you

WHAT YOU
SHOULD DO

It's the validity within your actions

Acting in the role of his better half

Without the title

Loyalty embodied is the foundation you've set

Towards a man and his history

Without fluidity beyond casual sex

But, you do it the best

Catering inhibitions because you yourself can't commit

It's a switch being flipped

Allowing him to hit without the emotional attachment

Detaches the aspects of femininity that's necessary

So the law of attraction remains active

And these niggas will never really care

Until you demand respect for the thing that got them there

DIALOGUE

The progression from boy to man is usually determined by an act of courage or defiance. Up until this point, I was defiant against all odds. It was easy because anything gained was accepted by the family (especially when they considered the trials I overcame). It was when I wanted more than the clichés that epitomize mediocrity I encountered difficulty. I started to foresee life beyond anguish and evolve from the boy I was into the man I am.

IN MY SLEEP

Blood on your hands leaves a spiritual residue

Because physically you've anticipated something to occur

But no one has implied, asked, or cared to figure out what you did

So the guilt fuels & incites the awareness that stains you

Leaving apart of you dead as another awakens

"Yo Don"

"Ya Donny?"

"You know I ain't gone say shit to nobody when we get back home"

"Who said you were going home?" "BANG"

In the end, the pain you embody must die in order for you to grow.

The crimes against you will never be acknowledged in nominal value,

so you can't carry things no one can see...

Donny had to die for Don to be free.

CHAPTER 4

OCCULT POWER OF THE
THIRD EYE

STUDENT OF THE GAME

Maturity is a forfeit of flesh

A cancellation of outside noise

While you're mental fortitude takes the test

Ironically mothers teach

That females advance quickly

While my intellect dangles against my ego

My mother never gave me the inside scoop

A lot of shit is you vs you

Like mama said, "Get outchea own way"

Stubborn, I'm steadfast against the tide

In attempt to move the elements to my will

It's like being a fish with no gills

I'm meant for the world but without knowledge how can I live

I guess by second hand thrills and hip hop appeals

But I'm cool on clubs and pills

I want more

Masa Musa, Fred Hampton, Jay Morrison

3 generations of black excellence is a quick

steal vs exploitation of us on screen in a portrayal of "real"

I still hear her saying, "Get outchea own way"

So a mentor I search for to learn more

Closing my mouth so my ears open more doors

I can't expect excellence from the same wars

Blaming the white man like this phone isn't the search

bar to greatness

If I get out my own way

This would then be a race

Just a student of the game up for the chase

MLK'S DREAM

In honor of MLK,

let me say that the unification of people will not transpire

until we acknowledge what we're taught to hate

Within our race we're deprived from the reality that

African American is not our nationality

Moorish ancestry outlines our souls

But a lot of "US" is what they stole

Even the definition of American, derives from the

aboriginals with copper faces

The Goddess Europa granted Europe its name

And Hip Hop became white washed when mass media retracted

the message and told us that we're "super predators"

See the agenda is to substitute the culture with distractions

that eliminates influence

But I'm not here to preach though

I just want you to acknowledge that similar to our radical

forefathers, we too are searching for an out

But this cannot happen if only one of us is willing to open our mouth

UNCHAINING THE TRADITION

Gentrification is only the foundation

That sets the separation

Between legit and discrete criminality

Out of your personality to remain blue collar

And sustain the inheritance of your hustling forefathers

So comprehension takes a precedence

Because now you know even with your 4yr degree

Nothing much has changed

The struggle has transcended with your knowledge

As you acknowledge that the rat race is a wheel

With its momentum fulfilled each time your linear income

gives you a biweekly thrill

With bad habits in tow the weekend is the only portion

of the week you know

Only to avoid the answers to a cyclic tradition

Your dreams become memories the day you begin to miss them

So don't dare forget them, overcome the opposition

and go get them

THEE BLACK PANTHERS

J Edgar Hoover's life embodies the vacuums we utilize

Because he sucked the integrity of our black faces through

fictitious investigations & slander

Disemboweled the panther and converted it back into the puddy

cat its supporters derived from

I die some when I think of Huey and his incarceration

Unlawfully shackled, deserted, yet still a King against scoundrels

with clubs in a hell

When freed....

Was converted into a fiend a thug a thief

A revolutionary died behind bars knowing atrocities

we don't dare to speak

Black Messiah please speak

"You can jail a revolutionary but you can't jail a revolution"

21 years of age

Hoover sent mercenaries to murder

The F in the Fuck You the Federal eye Hampton was the last hope

Because Eldridge fled and attempted to delegate matters he could no longer over see

Thus meticulously Wakanda was brought to its knees

It was reminiscent to Thanos wiping half the universe clean

except it was only the heroes that died in this scene

Now fast forward to 2018

Marvel's Black Panther is marvelous on the box office screen

But what we didn't see is the blank panthers amongst

the ones in the trees

My people please never forget your foundation because these

men allowed us to make it

UMOJI

Self-hatred gone be our genocide
Buying shit to make us feel good inside
Mislead by the media's perception that we consume and don't learn
See my verbiage is gone be real direct
See we buy shit to suppress other black folk while simultaneously
uplifting self
For example, you peep homeboy he been staring at you all night?
Cause you got the new Mikes and his shit really ain't that nice
See the assumption that materialistic items make me better than you
skews your frontal view
Detouring yourself-advancements to body enhancements
Searching for a new you
This is a concept that you scroll through
With each unconscious like
Idolizing what you want to be like
When it's ok to...just...be...YOU!

SETTLING FOR LESS

If your drive doesn't match your admirations to achieve

An alteration in the dream must occur

Because ideally we live by a materialistic standard in fear

of visual mediocrity

But the bank account doesn't match so there's the bigger hypocrisy

We settle for more than what we can afford

With a mindset that possessions

Will possess the confidence necessary to substitute what we lack

Why settle for the mistakes of the tree

When the apple is suppose to eat

See patience is key

Living with your vision attached to your very being

Means the dumb shit will never intervene with you and the cream

Don't alter your dreams

Adjust your current landscape to obtain these things

And I promise you'll settle for greatness instead of minor things

MONETARY GAINS

I see the money like lack of knowledge in the streets

A lethal appetite that's only satisfied when you eat

Gradual imperfections by your perspective of what it is

But when you get the arena in which you dwell is

fictional under your control

The Midas touch grasp on a bag

Entitlement in which you deem is relative to you

"I GET MONEY"

While money really got you

Cheese chasing in a rat race

Where most hustling don't see 22

I see the money like lack of knowledge in the streets

A lethal agenda that misperceives

Daydreaming cashing 401Ks

While working M-S just trying to make it and get paid

"I GET MONEY"

But at what expense

Because in this game you gotta give to get

And earn your keep

Neglect to buy land because clothes are cheap

Only to prove to another person identical that you're better

"BUT YOU GET MONEY THOUGH"

Ya nigga whatever

YOU'VE BEEN A QUEEN
BEFORE IG

You sell moments instead of own em, projecting

sensory to the classless

With the perception of depth

But you're deaf to what you project

Out in Cali slinging silicone in Silicon Valley

Adopting new nationalities, while yo black kids learn from the

mother that raised you better

See the white man is clever,

Dehumanize the black man make his woman self-conscious

Then provide labels as an intermittent to help them to flaunt it

But you stay on the gram tho

Reckless character with each post

What portion of your physique besides the pussy

the world don't know

Exercise your mind and not the hopeless ideals you inject in your rear

Because your insecurities with self only make it hard

for the real women here

The ones that work two jobs school full time single moms....I salute you.....no IG chick can do what you do

IN REFLECTION

My reflection has always been a hue of past transgressions

that hollowed my point of view

A distant mindset that unconsciously severs the conception of reality

Until...I heard "Daddy!" Like sudden impact

I'm jarred with emotion as I watch moments come into fruition

Movements that seem minuscule gather momentum then repetition

Growth before my eyes

My child is truly mine

An embodiment of my spirit at the time of conception

Looking directly at my reflection only outlines my flaws

As unexpected lessons I should've learned

Hypocrisy as I scold them when I still burn

Hits blunt slow burn

Because that's what It is

Raising children isn't quick

It's a challenge of how to fit the majority "of what to know"

within a 18 year stent

In hopes you don't miss shit

SPERM DONOR

I'm embarrassed to equate your existence to being a parent

And it's not the child support by the way

It's your meager attempt to provide on a monthly base that doesn't

substantiate to what I have to face

I'm like a continuous sub

That doesn't receive the credit for the dub

But I keep making the cut

Because raising a child is a profession that requires you to give

and not expect to receive

It's the watering of the seed

And in your case the reassurance the apple falls far from the tree

It's idiotic to me that you don't connect

Not scholastically, athletically, or emotionally

BUT! Black man to black man

I'm not your threat only an assist

For you to understand all the things you've missed

If it's all for her betterment let's be a team

Because only sperm donors cum with the initiative to leave

X3

It's a defining moment

A moment that doesn't seek compatibility

Is unmeasurable with intensity that fear populates

Are you okay? Is she okay? Am I okay?

As I catch my footing

Child #1 the calm before the storm

Wynne's birth nearly killed T blood at my feet

Transfused to stop the bleed

We all can breathe

On to Child #2 cultivated in my prime exempt from the arrogance

Adoni had me planted as I awaited

Arms out the King's arrival

Give me my son my child

It's almost an illusion gaining continuation of play

I scored but I got fouled anyway at the free throw line

contemplating the next play

That was 2016! Now we in

Adoni 15 months and I'm 28

Been hell since the first doctor visit

Yet his eyes give life the worth to keep living

Anal stenosis

Reflux

He's underweight Becomes delayed So we tube feed Do PT

And he starts to cut the corner

Gains some pounds

Tubes out

And Donny finally crawls

Shit was cool until last March when we got hit with

his most recent blood results

I don't remember shit but the words I heard 4yrs prior with

our very first child

"Tetrasomy 9P" In my 3rd child

Reluctant to cry In front of white folk

I cried in the car where my soul broke

It's almost an illusion gaining continuation of play I scored but I got

fouled anyway at the free throw line contemplating the next play

Just a couple months later I'm still in the same place

Test after test to make sure he straight

Only one more thing to face a blood test for me....

to see if I too am times 3

CLUB 2929

*The progression of a man is contingent upon
his ability to learn from other men*

Behind the ritualistic dap and RNS tats
"Shelby days" have a designated place in the lore of
DFG
The humble beginnings of the misfits
With admirations to get paid and fuck bitches
Evolved into a brotherhood against the white offensive
Harmonizing "crew love" into a mantra of self-love for the
contributions of one another
That was when we stopped calling each other nigga and
began saying "my brother"
As time progressed so did we
Lucrative amenities to portray what we really wanted to achieve
As we explored every segment of the scene
We left RNS to become DFG Like the soldiers we were
Friendly fire was only growing pains compared to the ballistic
reports from our aim

Unified by poverty the sovereignty derives from our need

of one another

But "Govern thyself when absent from your brother"

So when individual motives took a precedence we all got the

notion it's time to grow

Despite the path we each embody we still walk proudly knowing

that we always have one another

Still cherishing the moment we stopped calling each other nigga

and began saying "my brother"

Without these men I wouldn't be who I am today. I would like to thank each of them. Will, Mitch, Nell, Ced, Q, Drew, and B. 2 to da sky and RNS until we die.

TRIBUTE LETTER

Dear Ma,

First let's clear the air & let me say this is weird. How did I find myself doing what you taught me to do? It reminds me of the time you bought my first journal. Do you remember? I wrote in it every day. No poetry then so when you found it and read all the curse words you were pissed. You were so upset because you gave me the freedom to say whatever I wanted and I actually did. I still curse Ma, just not as much as I used to lol. Especially, not in my writing. I hope you can see it...the light that is. My words are no longer dark or possess the anger I once held. Nevertheless, to continue the transparency we've always had, I must apologize Ma. Because before you died I resented you for staying with Marcus after he hit you the first time. I never understood how you could be the strongest woman I know & yet succumb to a man that didn't amount to half of who you were. Overtime, I realized that you were terrified and did everything in your power to protect us. Even at times putting yourself in harm's way to deflect his attention from me to you. Ma, I really just want you to know I forgive you for everything that you couldn't do.

I find myself in constant question of the path that's been bestowed upon me as it relates to my past. "I never had a father", sounds so cliché but yet original when I think of the dilemma I face as a father being raised primarily by women. The constant questioning of one's manhood in comparison to other men has always troubled my psyche. Because you couldn't validate me as a man so you unconsciously taught me the ways of a woman. Thus, being organized and diligent in anything I attempted was considerably easy. But, being honorable and a leader of other men is something I had to learn. Overall, I'm grateful. I'm grateful because I had you as a mother and no one else. Thank you Ma for everything you did do. Within time I'll accomplish everything you didn't have enough time to conquer.

Your eldest son,
Donny

Dear Mom,

It's so many things I want to say to you face to face. I know I need to let these emotions out because honestly I'm not happy. I'm angry, hurt, depressed, and lost. When you died I lost myself and I couldn't find any remnants of who I was. Yes, you taught us self-confidence with the poem "I Am Somebody" but I didn't feel like I was somebody when you died. I'm angry because I still have flashbacks of my 11th birthday when you told me you were coming home from the hospital and you never did. I know I was young but I told you the dream I had about you. I saw your grave, I saw the date, and I saw mines too. But, you brushed it off and told me don't worry about it. I'm hurt because at a young age I had to deal with a lot of things that affected me. Seeing you in chemo hurt me so much. Seeing you cry because of the pain and wishing it would stop. But, then tell me everything was going to be okay and it wasn't! How was everything is going to be alright? When you died, Dad came and acted like he was always in our life. He tried to flip it on you for why we couldn't see him. I struggled to have a relationship with him. He told me so many things about you that I knew wasn't true. He would tell me all these hurtful things. He would say he hated me and the reason why he hit me is because I looked like you. I went through a lot after your death. Dad's side of the family would try to make it seem like it was my fault you died because of my rebellious attitude. But, I thought I was a good kid I stayed out of trouble I just hated them and the situation I was in. I wanted to run away, I wanted to kill myself anything to get away from them. Why couldn't you just stay with us? Why did you have to leave us when we ALL NEEDED YOU THE MOST? I didn't have a mother figure in my life and I did so many things I regret and I knew was wrong because I didn't have anybody. I was by myself trying to survive. I didn't get taught the things I was supposed to get taught by you so I could be strong like you. I don't know who I am or what I'm capable of. All I know is that we had great memories. At graduation and the baby shower I just wanted you nobody else. I wanted to hear that I was doing well, it's okay if you fall just get back up, and don't be afraid to show your feelings. Now I'm lost and my soul is dark. I put this smile on my face like everything is okay and deep down it's not. I just want to be happy. If you can come to my dreams when I need you the most it'll be the best thing in life to hear you say it'll be okay one last time......

Your youngest,

Sandy